Countries of the World

Nigeria

by Kristin Thoennes

Consultant:
A. A. Musa
Senior Consul
Embassy of the Federal Republic of Nigeria

Bridgestone Books
an imprint of Capstone Press
Mankato, Minnesota

Bridgestone Books are published by Capstone Press
151 Good Counsel Drive, P.O. Box 669, Mankato, Minnesota, 56002
http://www.capstone-press.com

Library of Congress Cataloging-in-Publication Data
Thoennes, Kristin.
    Nigeria/by Kristin Thoennes.
    p.   cm.—(Countries of the world)
    Includes bibliographical references and index.
    Summary: Discusses the landscape, people, animals, food, sports, and culture of the country
of Nigeria.
    ISBN 0-7368-0154-5
    1. Nigeria—Juvenile literature. [1. Nigeria.] I. Title. II. Series: Countries of the world
(Mankato, Minn.)
    DT515.22.T49   1999
    966.9—dc21   98-36964
                                                                                      CIP
                                                                                      AC

Editorial Credits
Blanche R. Bolland, editor; Timothy Halldin, cover designer; Linda Clavel and Timothy Halldin,
    illustrators; Kimberly Danger and Sheri Gosewisch, photo researchers

Photo Credits
Beryl Goldberg, 8
The Hutchison Library, 14, 18
Jason Lauré, 5 (bottom), 10
Photri-Microstock, 20
StockHaus Limited, 5 (top)
Valan Photos/Van and Alan Williamson, 6, 12, 16
Victor Englebert, cover

Table of Contents

Fast Facts

Name: Federal Republic of Nigeria

Capital: Abuja

Population: More than 107 million

Languages: English, Hausa, Yoruba, Ibo

Religions: Islam, Christianity

Size: 356,669 square miles (923,773 square kilometers)

Nigeria is more than twice the size of the U.S. state of California.

Crops: Cocoa, palm oil, corn, yams

Maps

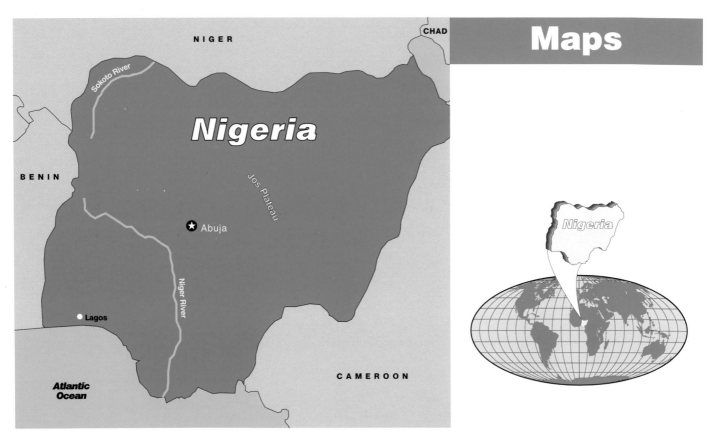

4

Flag

Nigeria's flag has three vertical stripes. A light green stripe lies on each end. A white stripe is in the middle. The green stripes on the flag stand for farming. The white stripe stands for oneness and peace.

Currency

The unit of currency in Nigeria is the naira. One hundred kobo equal 1 naira.

In the late 1990s, about 86 naira equaled 1 U.S. dollar. About 57 naira equaled 1 Canadian dollar.

The Land

Nigeria is a country in western Africa. The Atlantic Ocean meets Nigeria's western coastline. The Sahara Desert lies to the north.

Brown grasses and small trees cover the flat land of northern Nigeria. Grassy hills roll across the middle part of Nigeria. The Jos Plateau (pla-TOH) lies in the center of the country. This high land is flat on top.

Rain forests grow in southern Nigeria. Up to 150 inches (381 centimeters) of rain fall there each year. Swamps lie near the ocean. Bushy trees grow in this wet, spongy area.

Nigeria has two seasons. The rainy season lasts from April through September. More rain falls in southern Nigeria than in the north. The dry season lasts for the rest of the year. Nigeria's climate is hot year round. Temperatures range from about 65°F to 100°F (18°C to 38°C).

Grassy hills cover the middle part of Nigeria.

The People

Hundreds of different groups of people live in Nigeria. Each group has its own language and takes pride in its way of life.

Two large groups make their homes in the north. Many Hausas (HOW-suhs) are traders. Some Fulanis (foo-LAHN-ees) are farmers. Other Fulanis live in tents and often move to find grass for their animals. Most northern Nigerians follow the Islam religion. They are called Muslims.

Most southern Nigerians are Christian. The Yorubas (YAW-ruh-buhs) live mostly in the southwest. Many Yorubas farm or fish. The Ibo (EE-boh) is the largest group in the southeast. Many Ibos work in business and government.

Some Nigerians live in walled compounds. The group of homes in a compound share a yard. Nigerian men often have several wives. Each wife has her own house in the compound.

Some Nigerians live in walled compounds.

Going to School

Nigerian children begin grade school at age 6. After third grade, teachers speak English in class. Some children go to secondary school at age 12. Students study math, reading, and science. They also study handwriting and languages.

Nigerian schoolchildren wear uniforms. Girls wear a jumper or skirt with a blouse. Boys wear a shirt and shorts.

School buildings are different in cities and in the country. Classes in cities are in large buildings. In the countryside, teachers often hold classes in one-room schools or outside.

Some children in the countryside attend bush schools. Students there learn the history and ways of their people. Men teach boys how to hunt, make tools, and care for animals. Women teach girls about cooking and crafts. Girls also learn how to take care of people who are sick.

Some classes take place outside in the shade.

Nigerian Food

Most Nigerians like spicy food. Cooks add peppers and spices to food that does not have much flavor. Rice is a main part of many Nigerian meals.

People in northern Nigeria eat tuwo. They often eat this smooth grain mixture with a vegetable sauce. The sauce consists of onions, tomatoes, okra, and sometimes beef.

People in southern Nigeria eat gari and yams. Cooks pound and then boil cassava roots to make gari. Nigerians also peel, boil, and pound yams. They then roll this vegetable into balls. A spicy sauce adds flavor to both gari and yams. Southern Nigerians near the ocean eat a lot of seafood.

Kola fruits grow on trees in Nigeria. People cut out the nuts from inside the fruit. Many Nigerians like to chew on kola nuts.

Nigerians buy yams at outdoor markets.

Nigerian Clothing

Some Nigerians wear clothes like North Americans wear. Others wear different types of clothing. Colorful clothes with patterns are popular in Nigeria. Many Nigerians like how the bright colors look when people dance.

Nigerian women wrap cloths around their lower bodies. They wear loose blouses. Loose clothes are more comfortable in Nigeria's hot weather. Women often wear scarves on their heads. Large necklaces and earrings are popular.

Nigerian men favor long shirts or gowns and baggy pants. Some men wear small, round caps called fezzes.

Children's clothing helps keep them cool. Girls wear cotton dresses. Boys wear shorts. Some Nigerian children in the countryside do not wear any clothes.

Colorful clothes with patterns are popular.

Animals

Many wild animals roam Nigeria's countryside. Lions, leopards, and hyenas hunt in the north. Antelopes graze on grasses there. The Niger River is home to crocodiles and hippopotomuses. Monkeys and chimpanzees live in the rain forests of southern Nigeria.

Camels are common in the dry north. These large animals can go long periods of time without water. Nigerians often ride camels instead of horses. Camels also carry goods.

Birds live throughout Nigeria. Quail and vultures are common everywhere. Parrots live in southern Nigeria. Egrets nest near the coast.

Nigeria once had more animals. The number of elephants and giraffes has dropped sharply. People hunted and killed these animals. A wildlife preserve in central Nigeria keeps animals safe. Animals there live as they do in the wild.

Monkeys live in the rain forests in southern Nigeria.

Sports and Games

Nigerians enjoy many sports. Horseback riding is popular in the north. Camel and horse racing are other favorite sports in northern Nigeria. Nigerians in the south often enter canoe races.

Some sports are favorites all over Nigeria. Boxing and wrestling are popular. Many Nigerians enjoy watching soccer. Nigeria's soccer team won a gold medal at the 1996 Olympic Games.

Ayu is a popular game in Nigeria. Players use stones, beans, or seeds in this game. They move these pieces across rows of holes on boards. Nigerians sometimes make holes in rocks or in the ground to play ayu.

Many Nigerians like to dance. Dancing can be more than just fun. This activity can teach children how to be adults by telling a story. Traditional dances also tell about life long ago.

Traditional dancing is popular in Nigeria.

Celebrations

Many Nigerians celebrate the same holidays as North Americans. One of those holidays is Christmas. Children wear masks and paint their faces for this holiday. Nigerians have dancing and drumming contests on Christmas.

Nigerians also celebrate New Year's Day. They blow horns and dance in the streets. Parties sometimes last two or three days.

Nigeria's Fishing Festival is in February. Men with nets jump into the Sokoto River in northwestern Nigeria. They each try to catch the most fish. Nigerians also have swimming and canoeing races during the Fishing Festival.

National Day is October 1 in Nigeria. Nigerians celebrate their freedom on this day. People decorate with green and white. These are the colors of the Nigerian flag. Nigerians dance and listen to music. Children dress in costumes.

Many Nigerians compete in the Fishing Festival.

Hands On: Play Lion and the Lamb

Nigerian children play the game Lion and the Lamb. You can learn to play this game.

<u>What You Need</u>
Five or more players

<u>What You Do</u>
1. Choose someone to be the lion.
2. Choose someone to be the lamb.
3. Have the other children form a circle. They should join hands and cross legs with the person next to them.
4. Have the lamb stand inside the circle.
5. Have the lion try to break through the circle to get the lamb. The players in the circle try to keep the lion out.

Learn to Speak Yoruban

good-bye	o dabo	(OH DAH-BAW)
good morning	ku aro	(KOO RAW)
long time no see	o t'ojo meta	(OH TAW-GAW MAY-TAH)
no	oti	(OH-TEE)
please	jo	(GAW)
thank you	o se	(OH SHAY)
yes	beni	(BEN-EE)

Words to Know

cassava (keh-SAW-veh)—a plant that grows in hot climates; Nigerians eat the roots of the cassava.
compound (KOM-pound)—a walled-in area with a group of houses that share a yard
plateau (pla-TOH)—an area of high, flat land
wildlife preserve (WILDE-life pri-ZURV)—an area set aside to protect animals
yam (YAM)—the root from a vine that grows in the tropics; Nigerians often eat yams with a spicy sauce.

Read More

Adeeb, Hassan, and Bonnetta Adeeb. *Nigeria: One Nation, Many Cultures.* Exploring Cultures of the World. Tarrytown, N.Y.: Benchmark Books, 1996.

Owhonda, John. *Nigeria: A Nation of Many Peoples.* Discovering Our Heritage. Parsippany, N. J.: Dillon Press, 1998.

Useful Addresses and Internet Sites

Embassy of the Federal Republic of Nigeria
1333 16th Street NW
Washington, DC 20036

Permanent Mission of Nigeria to the United Nations
828 Second Avenue, 20th floor
New York, NY 10017

Motherland Nigeria
http://www.motherlandnigeria.com
Nigeria.Com
http://www.nigeria.com

Index